Movie World

Colin Millar and Spike Breakwell

Contents

Introduction – 2

A History of Film – 4

Animated Films – 10

A World of Movies – 14

Making Pictures – 30

Movies for Everyone – 42

Glossary – 44

Index – 45

Introduction

Whether it was around a campfire in the middle of the desert, in the evening in a town square or in the hall of a Viking warrior, people have always loved to tell and listen to stories. Stories offer an escape from everyday life. People can imagine themselves as the hero or heroine and do things that they would never have the chance to do in reality.

Films are another way of telling and sharing stories. They allow people to spend time in another world or place. They can be funny, sad, exciting or interesting. They can be enjoyed alone or in good company. The whole family, young and old, can all find something to enjoy in the same film.

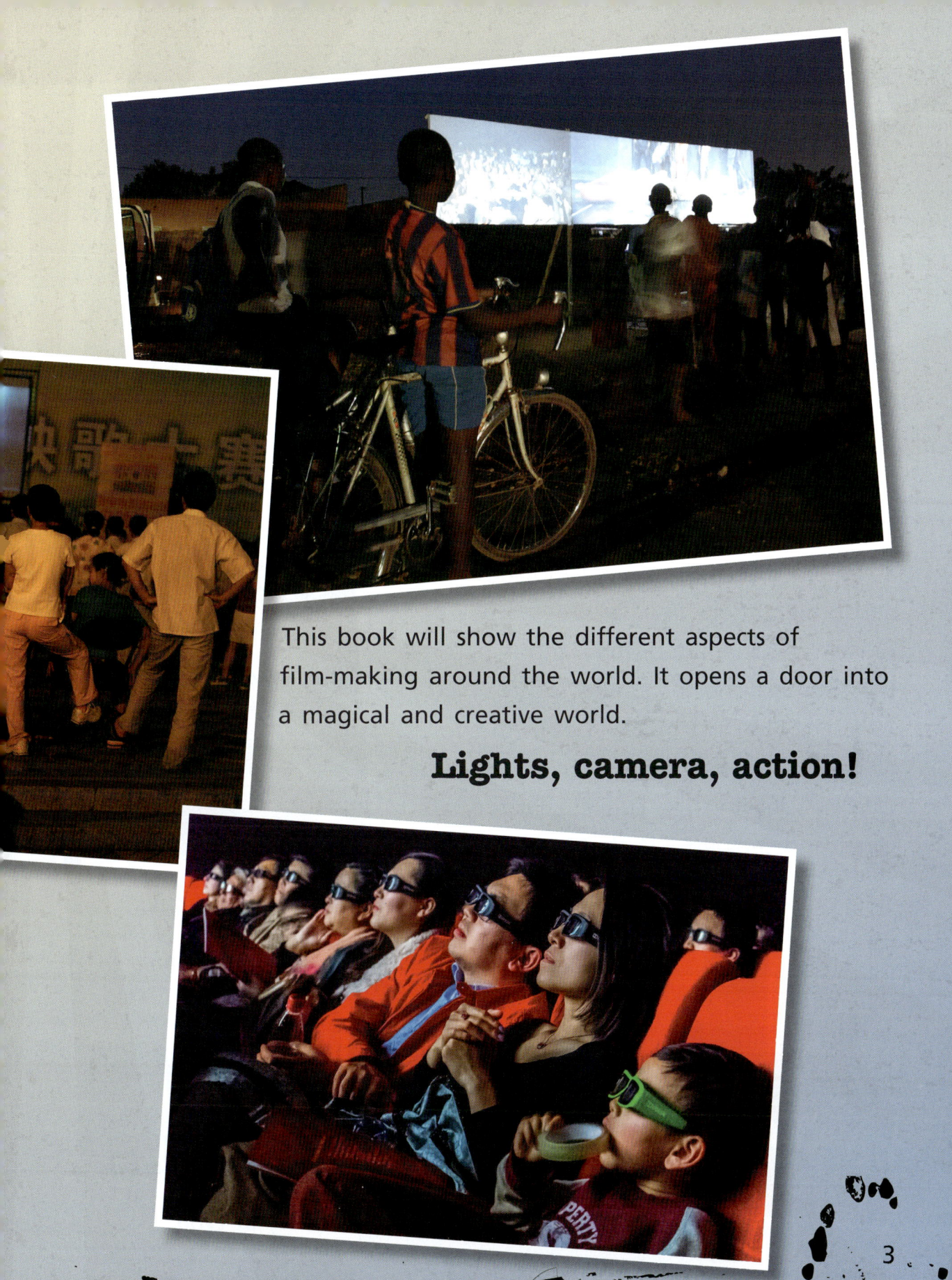

This book will show the different aspects of film-making around the world. It opens a door into a magical and creative world.

Lights, camera, action!

A History of Film

The Camera: An invention that changed the world

Today, movies are shown across the world, in many different languages and styles. But where did this worldwide **industry** come from? Who were the **innovators** of film and who were the stars of their movies?

The history of film begins with Louis and Auguste Lumiere, who lived in Lyon, France. In 1894, the brothers designed and built a camera that could record moving images and **project** them onto a screen. They called it a Cinematographe and it became the standard movie camera for the next 25 years. The first movie shot with this camera followed a year later. It was called 'Workers leaving the Lumiere Factory at Lyon' and showed just that.

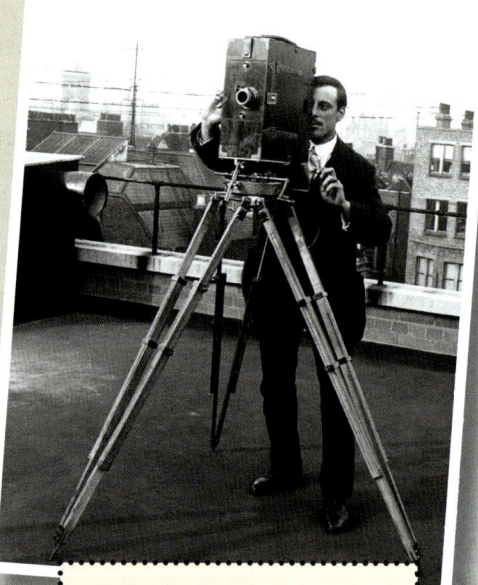

This is an early Cinematographe. The operator had to turn a handle to make the camera work.

a scene from 'Workers leaving the Lumiere Factory at Lyon'

In 1902, a French movie maker, Georges Melies, created a movie called 'Voyage to the Moon'. It used **special effects** and it introduced colour to the screen by using hand-painted images. For many years, Georges' movie was thought to be the best ever made, and other movie makers copied his ideas.

FILM FACTS

The word 'movie' is short for 'moving pictures'. Until 1895, people had only seen 'still pictures' called photographs.

George Melies hand-drawing his early animated film

Four years later, the first animated cartoon was produced. It was drawn and filmed by J. Stuart Blackton and was called 'Humorous Phases of Funny Faces'. Later, other animators, like Walt Disney, followed his example.

Only 16 years after the invention of the movie camera, there was a worldwide movie industry.

FILM FACTS

Movies made before 1927 were silent. No one had worked out how to record and play back sound to fit the movie. Early cinemas had a piano player providing music to go with the film.

First of the Movie Stars

Charlie Chaplin was one of the very first film stars. Chaplin was born in London in 1889. His family were poor, and Chaplin had to start working on the stage when he was still a young child. His life changed in 1913 when he was asked to go and act in America.

American film producers saw Chaplin acting on the stage and offered him the chance to act on camera. Chaplin developed a comedy character called The Tramp, wearing a moustache, baggy trousers and big shoes for the role. Playing The Tramp made him one of Hollywood's first big silent movie stars. Charlie played the role for over 20 years, in dozens of films such as 'The Kid', 'Gold Rush' and 'City Lights'. He went on to become a major film producer. Chaplin's silent movies continued to be successful, long after films with sound had been developed.

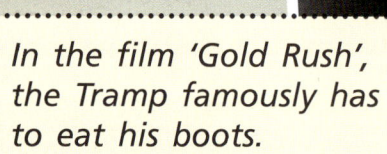

In the film 'Gold Rush', the Tramp famously has to eat his boots.

'The Talkies'

The first words ever heard by a cinema audience were, *'Wait a minute, wait a minute, you ain't heard nothing yet!'* The 1927 film was called 'The Jazz Singer'. The ability to play back sound alongside the images in a film introduced a new era in film making.

The arrival of 'The Talkie', as the new talking pictures were called, let audiences hear the lines spoken by the actors and allowed film makers to tell much more interesting stories.

In the 1930s, the Talkies were enjoyed by many. Thanks to this popularity and full colour movies like 'Snow White and the Seven Dwarfs', film-making **exploded**. Millions of people dreamed of becoming actors, and living a life of fame and fortune. Thousands travelled from all over the world to the **studios** in Hollywood but only very few became movie stars.

the poster for the first 'Talkie'

FILM FACTS

Before 'The Jazz Singer', film makers and directors had to display actors lines and plot explanations on caption boards.

Movies Across the World

People all around the world wanted to tell their stories. Countries such as China, Japan, Malaysia and Nigeria began to produce their own movies. In India, for example, Bombay (now known as Mumbai) became a centre of movie-making excellence. The industry in Bombay became known as Bollywood after the studios in Hollywood.

Bollywood movies are quite different in style and content to the western movies, often using song and dance to **portray** the story. Their movies can be funny, **tragic** and moving all at once.

'Raja Harishchandra' by Dadasaheb Phalke was released in 1913. It is thought to be the first silent **feature film** made in India. Some of the most famous and **epic** movies of Indian cinema were produced between the late 1940s and the 1960s, including 'Mother India' (1957), which was **nominated** for the Academy Award (called an Oscar) for Best Foreign Language Film.

Bollywood films are still famous for their colourful costumes and dancing.

Meena Kumari

Meena Kumari was one of the most famous actresses in early Bollywood movies. She was born in 1932 in Bombay, India. Her birth name was Begum Mahjabeen Bux. She learned to act and dance when she was very young.

Meena appeared in her first film aged just six years old. She played Baby Meena in the 1939 film 'Leatherface'. She changed her name to Meena Kumari in 1952, when she appeared in the film 'Baiju Bawra'.

Meena's best-known film is 'Pakeezah' which took 14 years to complete. Unfortunately, Meena did not live to see the film become a huge hit. She died in 1972, just as the film was released.

Meena Kumari

poster for the movie 'Pakeezah'

Animated Films

The first animations were not specifically created for children. They were enjoyed by everyone.

Walt Disney is one of the best-known animators and creators of cartoon movies in the history of film making. In 1928, he produced his first short animation film which was called 'Steamboat Willie'. At first, the little mouse in this animation was called Willie. In later films, Disney changed the name to Mickey Mouse. Disney's first full length feature film 'Snow White and the Seven Dwarfs' was released in 1937.

Walt Disney

Steamboat Willie, later known as Mickey Mouse

Snow White and the Seven Dwarfs

Many of Disney's movies have some common themes. They are often based on **fairy tales** from around the world and usually involve overcoming difficulties to find happiness.

Today, many great animated films are made each year. However, the use of **computer graphics (CGI)** means that animators no longer have to hand-draw every frame of film.

Finding Nemo

Anime: Japan's Fantastic Cartoon Makers

Japanese animation, called Anime in Japan, is as old as the film industry. Starting as far back as the early 1900's, the oldest surviving Anime is 'Namakura Gatana', meaning Blunt Sword. Japanese animators like fast-paced action and **fantastical** characters. They can also portray very touching stories where children find ways to overcome **adversity**.

One beautifully animated film is 'My Neighbour Totoro' released in 1988. Like most films made by Miyazaki's Studio Ghibli, this family film has a powerful **ecological** theme.

Tortoro and Satsuki wait for the bus in the rain in a scene from 'My Neighbour Totoro.'

Japanese Anime continues to produce outstanding animations that transport the audience to amazing places and tell wonderfully imaginative stories.

Anime is very stylised. For example, characters have bigger eyes than usual. This allows for many emotions to be shown clearly through the eyes.

FILM FACTS

Animated 'shorts', as they are called, only last a few minutes but feature length movies and animation can last up to two hours.

an example of Anime's style of animation

A World of Movies

Hollywood, USA

Today, hundreds of movies are made all over the world. However, perhaps the most famous place for making movies is Hollywood, near Los Angeles in California.

Movies have been made in Hollywood for over 100 years. About 600 films are made there every year. The three highest-earning films of all time are: 'Avatar', 'Star Wars' and the 1939 epic 'Gone with the Wind'.

A film crew sets up lights and cameras for shooting.

There are six major film-making studios in Hollywood: Disney, Universal, Warner Brothers, Fox, Paramount, Columbia. They all offer exciting tours that attract tens of thousands of visitors every year.

Visitors can also see the Hollywood Walk of Fame. It features more than 2,600 five-pointed stars. They celebrate famous actors, actresses and directors.

Fans often leave flowers on the stars of their favourite actors.

Mickey Mouse's star

Woody Woodpecker

FILM FACTS

The cartoon characters Woody Woodpecker, Bugs Bunny and Mickey Mouse all have their own stars.

Hollywood Star

Steven Spielberg – Director

Born in 1946 in the United States of America, Steven Spielberg made several short films when he was still a child, using his father's film camera.

He became one of the youngest television directors for Universal Studios in the late 1960s. He made a film called 'Duel' for television. Movie makers saw this film and liked it. They gave him the chance to direct for the cinema.

His films often explore people's fears as in 'Jaws' (1975). Others explore the idea of visitors from outer space as in 'Close Encounters of the Third Kind' (1977) and 'E.T.' (1982).

Spielberg has become well-known for making blockbuster movies such as 'Raiders of the Lost Ark', and in 1993 'Jurassic Park', about an island where dinosaurs have been brought back to life.

Spielberg directed the 2011 animated film 'The Adventures of Tintin', based on the popular comic series by Hergé. However, it was his film version of 'War Horse' (2011) that won him most praise from critics and other film makers. The movie received six Academy Award nominations.

Bollywood, India

India produced its first film in 1899, 11 years before the first Hollywood movie. In the 1970s, Indian cinema overtook America as the place where the greatest number films are made. The film industry in India became known as 'Bollywood'.

Bollywood is estimated to employ over 300,000 people. There are 13 major studios, producing many, many movies.

'Do Aankhein Baraah Haath' is the first Indian film to have won the Golden Globe award.

The Filmfare Awards are the Bollywood equivalent of the Academy Awards (Oscars). There have been 62 ceremonies since the awards first started.

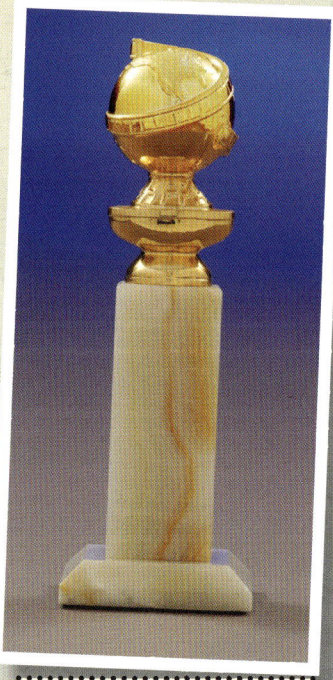

a Golden Globe

'Dilwale Dulhaniya Le Jayenge' is the longest running movie in the world. It has been running in cinemas for over 1000 weeks!

Bollywood dancers on the film set

Priyanka Chopra won a Filmfare award in 2016.

19

Bollywood Star

Salman Khan

Born in 1965, Salman Khan is an actor, producer, television personality and singer. He is one of the biggest stars in Bollywood.

He has been in the movie business for 30 years.

His acting **debut** was a supporting role in the 1988 film 'Biwi Ho To Aisi'. He was so good that he was given the lead role in his next movie.

His many awards include two National Film Awards as a producer, and two Filmfare Awards as an actor.

In 2011, he launched his own production company called SKBH Productions.

The first movie he made with SKBH was 'Chillar Party', which went on to win three National Awards, for Best Children's film, Best Original Screenplay and Child Artist's Award.

Nollywood, Nigeria

The first film in Nigeria was called 'Palaver' and was made in 1926.

However, Nigerian cinema did not really start to grow rapidly until the 1990s. This was when home video cameras became easier to buy in Nigeria. The movie industry became nicknamed "Nollywood", and for a short period in the 2000s, more films were being made in Nigeria than in Hollywood.

Safi Faye was the first African female director to become known around the world.

Nollywood Star

Genevieve Nnaji

Genevieve was born on May 3rd 1979 in Mbaise, Nigeria.

She started her acting career as a child actress in the then popular television series 'Ripples' at the age of eight.

In 1998, at the age of 19, she was introduced into the growing Nigerian film industry with the movie 'Most Wanted'.

In 2010, she starred in the award-winning film 'Ijé: The Journey'. In this film, Nnaji plays a young Nigerian woman travelling to the USA to help her sister.

Genevieve has received several awards and nominations for her work, including the Best Actress of the Year award at the 2001 City People Awards and the Best Actress in a Leading Role award at the 2005 Africa Movie Academy Awards.

As well as acting Genevieve can also sing.

FILM FACTS
Genevieve has appeared in over 80 films.

China

Cinema was introduced in China in 1896 and the first Chinese film, 'The Battle of Dingjunshan', was made in 1905.

China is now home to the largest film studio in the world, the Hengdian World Studios. In 2010, it had the third largest film industry by number of feature films produced annually.

the Hendian Studio complex

During the 1920s and 1930s, the Chinese film industry grew. The greatest Chinese director of this time was Fei Mu.

*This is a **still** from Fei Mu's most acclaimed film, 'Spring in a Small Town'.*

Zhang Yimou – Top of China's Directors

Zhang Yimou is one of China's top directors. He has won many awards from all over the world not just China. He has won awards at the Cannes film festival, Academy awards and elsewhere. His movie 'Hero' was one of the few foreign-language films to debut at number 1 at the American box office. He directed the opening and closing ceremonies of the 2008 Beijing Summer Olympic Games.

Chinese Star

Jackie Chan

Jackie Chan was born on 7 April 1954, in Hong Kong. His parents nicknamed him 'Cannonball' because he was always rolling around.

At eight years old, he appeared in the film 'Big and Little Wong Tin Bar', released in 1962.

In 1976, Jackie received a message from Willie Chan, a film producer in Hong Kong who had been impressed with Jackie's work. Willie Chan became Jackie's personal manager and firm friend, and has remained so for over 30 years. In 1995 Jackie appeared in 'Rumble in the Bronx', which is still very popular today.

Jackie Chan in action in 'Thunderbolt'

He is best known for his **martial arts** films, performing many stunts himself.

Jackie has been working in the movie industry for over fifty years. In his spare time, he runs charities for the poor in Hong Kong, and teaches at the Hong Kong Polytechnic University.

Jackie Chan uses his skills as a master of martial arts in many of his movies.

Japan

Movies were first produced in Japan in early 1897 by Inabata Katsutaro. The first successful film was shot later the same year and showed the sites of Tokyo. Early fims were heavily influenced by traditional theatre. They were silent, and narrators used to sit next to the screen to tell the audience what was happening.

The first female Japanese performer to appear in a film professionally was the dancer and actress Tokuko Nagai Takagi, who appeared in four American films between 1911 and 1914.

'The Captain's Daughter' was one of the first films with sound in Japan. It was released in 1917.

Japan became famous for Anime movies, and monster movies with characters, like Godzilla.

Tokuko Nagai Takagi, in her finest clothes

Child characters in Anime films have big, expressive eyes.

Japanese Star

Godzilla

In the 1950s to 1970s, Japanese movie-makers were monster-mad. They made dozens of movies about all kinds of monsters, but the most famous of all was Godzilla, a 100-metre tall monster who stamps through Tokyo.

Godzilla first appeared in 1954, in a *tokusatso* movie (meaning film with special effects). In the first film, Godzilla was played by an actor in a **latex** suit. The newest Hollywood version was made using CGI effects.

Making Pictures

The Movie Making Process

When a movie is made, most film makers follow the **method** outlined here.

1. Script writing and Storyboard

A film usually begins with someone having an idea of a story they want to tell. It could be a funny, sad, romantic or scary story. A scriptwriter takes this idea and writes a story around it. This is called the script.

The scriptwriter will describe what the audience will see on the screen. They will write where each scene is set, whether it takes place during the day or at night and, most importantly, what the actors will do and say. An artist will then be asked to draw each scene as a series of small cartoons. This is known as the storyboard.

FILM FACTS
The script may be written many times before everyone is happy.

The storyboard to a famous film. Guess which one.

2. Funding

The next step is an important one. In order to make the film, money must be found to cover the costs of filming and to pay the actors and crew. Filming can be very expensive. The person finding this money is called the producer. The producer might go to a number of different people and ask them to invest in the film. They will show them the storyboard and the script and say "This is a brilliant film we want to make. Will you help?" When the producer is happy that there is enough money available, the next stage in the process can begin.

3. Casting

Once a film has funding, the characters must be cast. This is when actors are chosen to act as the different people in the story. This usually happens at an audition. The director is in charge of what the film looks like. They will listen to an actor reading part of the script aloud. If the director likes it, the actor will be asked to play the character in the movie. If the director decides on a big star, he may have to hold up the start of filming until the star is ready. And really big stars demand big wages!

FILM FACTS

When the director says "Action!" they are telling the actors to begin doing what it says they are to do in the script.

an actor auditioning for a film role

4. Locations and Shooting Schedule

Once the actors have been chosen, the director and producer must decide where and when each scene is to be shot. The order the scenes are shot in is what is called the shooting schedule. A location finder will be asked to find suitable places to film scenes that cannot be filmed in a studio. Sometimes an outside place can be recreated indoors in a studio but it is usually better to film the real thing.

Sometimes movies require filming in the most difficult locations, like jungles or mountains.

5. Filming

Filming can take many weeks. Each scene is filmed from many different angles, with everyone making sure it is as good as it can be. The actors will have to say their words correctly, the lighting and the sound will have to be perfect and the camera operators will have to have filmed the action. All that work for just one scene!

6. Behind the camera

This is the director. She's very important. Her job is to make the film look good on screen. She helps decide how scenes are shot by planning who is in the scene and from what angle the scene is filmed.

This is the camera operator. It's his job to film while the actors are acting their parts in the film.

This is the lighting operator. Every scene is different and needs different lighting. Just as a sound person will put scary sound effects into a horror film, the lighting operator will make sure there are lots of shadows where the monsters can hide. It's like painting with light!

This is the sound operator. Unless it's silent, a film will need good sound. Actors need to be heard clearly, or the audience won't know what's going on.

Here is the key grip. Film sets often require lots of building, scaffolding and preparation work. The key grip is in charge of a team of grips who make sure the set is ready and everything needed for each scene is in place.

The boom swinger has the microphone attached to a very long pole. It's his job to get the microphone as near to the actors as possible without it being seen.

These are extras. They have no lines to speak, but they act out small parts while the camera focuses on the main actors and actresses. Some epic movies have thousands of extras.

7. Editing

After the action has been filmed, the director will work with a film editor to put the scenes in the correct order. In the early days of movie-making, this was done with scissors and glue, actually cutting the film up and sticking it together in a different order. Now it is done on computer.

8. Promotion

When the director and film editor are happy that the movie will look great and tells the story well, the producer will organise the promotion of the movie. This involves a variety of different things. A **trailer** is created, giving a brief glimpse of the movie which is shown in cinemas before the film is released. The stars and director may be asked to give interviews on TV, radio, newspapers and magazines. Advertisements will be taken out in newspapers and large posters called billboards will be put up in towns and cities. This is done to try to attract as big an audience as possible.

a billboard poster

9. The review

When a movie is released, it is important that people know what it is about and whether it is a good or a bad film. Journalists will see a film and write their opinions about it. A review can be both good or bad. Here is a review for a dinosaur movie.

Dinosaurs Don't Sing

The latest film release is the animated dinosaur comedy, 'Dinosaurs Don't Sing'. The story takes place in the Cretaceous era and follows a young T-Rex called Terry and his efforts to form a pop group with his dinosaur friends. His efforts are initially **thwarted** by his parents and the other older dinosaurs who can't or won't understand what the point of a pop group is.

Terry keeps going and the movie follows the group's adventures, triumphs and failures, with an ending that will leave viewers of all ages charmed and delighted. With a sound track of original songs by the rock group The Reapers, everyone will leave the cinema humming the tunes.

The animation is imaginative, bright and colourful without being fussy. The characters have a realism that has the viewer believing in them. What sets this film above others of its type is the script. It has jokes aimed at the younger viewers, yet it has enough jokes to keep the grown-ups entertained.

The lead actors, Dave McClure as Terry and Babette Moncur as Jenny the Stegosaurus, both excel themselves and genuinely sound like they had a great time voicing the characters. The performances lift this movie to new heights and give it such a warm feeling you'll leave the cinema glowing.

One minor fault that could be picked with this movie, is that Terry passed the problems in his way a little too easily. This doesn't, in general, spoil the movie in any way, but it holds it back a little.

All in all, this is a great family movie that will make you laugh out loud a lot, cry a little and have your feet tapping to the music. If you only see one animated film this year, make it this one.

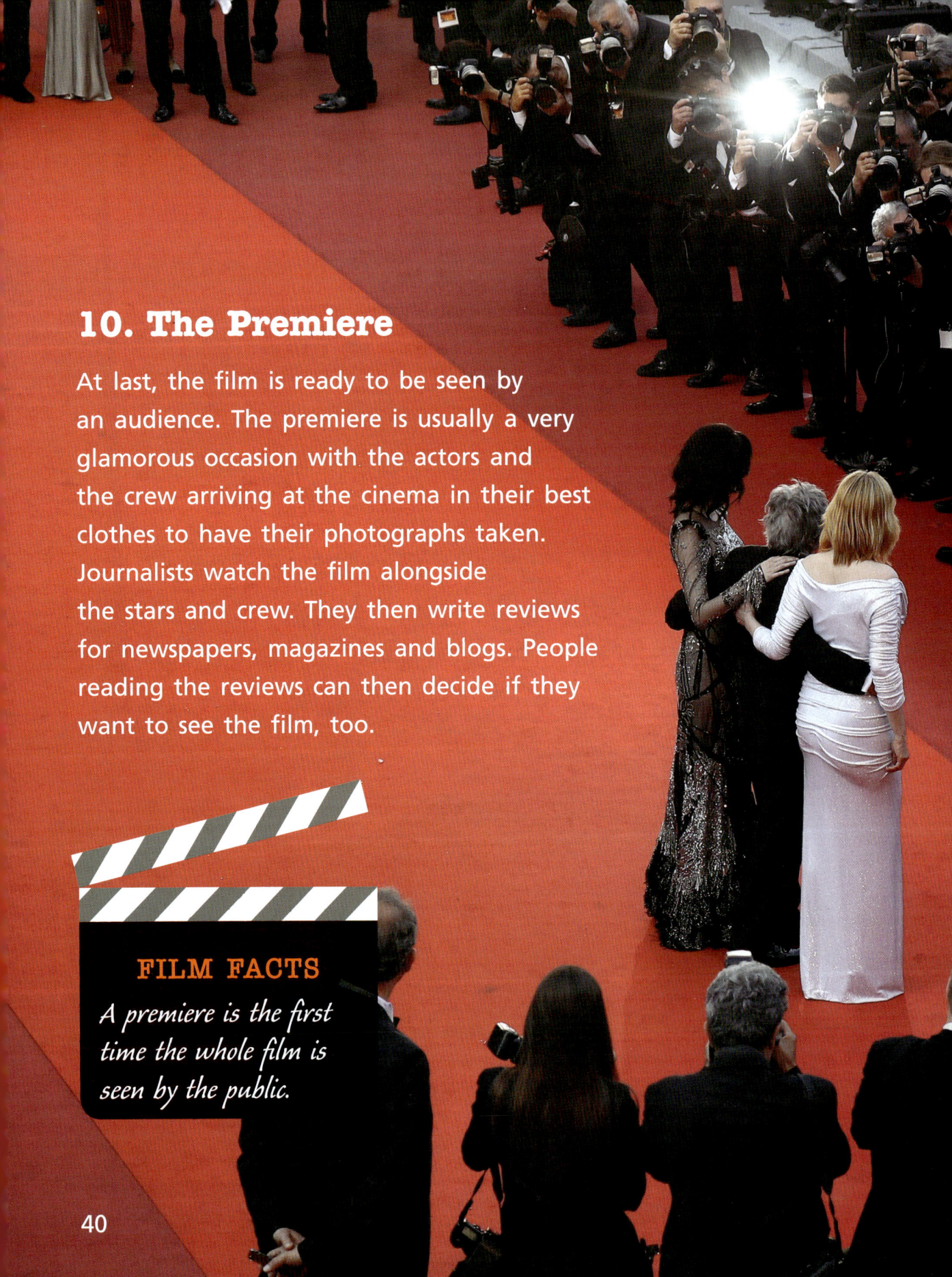

10. The Premiere

At last, the film is ready to be seen by an audience. The premiere is usually a very glamorous occasion with the actors and the crew arriving at the cinema in their best clothes to have their photographs taken. Journalists watch the film alongside the stars and crew. They then write reviews for newspapers, magazines and blogs. People reading the reviews can then decide if they want to see the film, too.

FILM FACTS

A premiere is the first time the whole film is seen by the public.

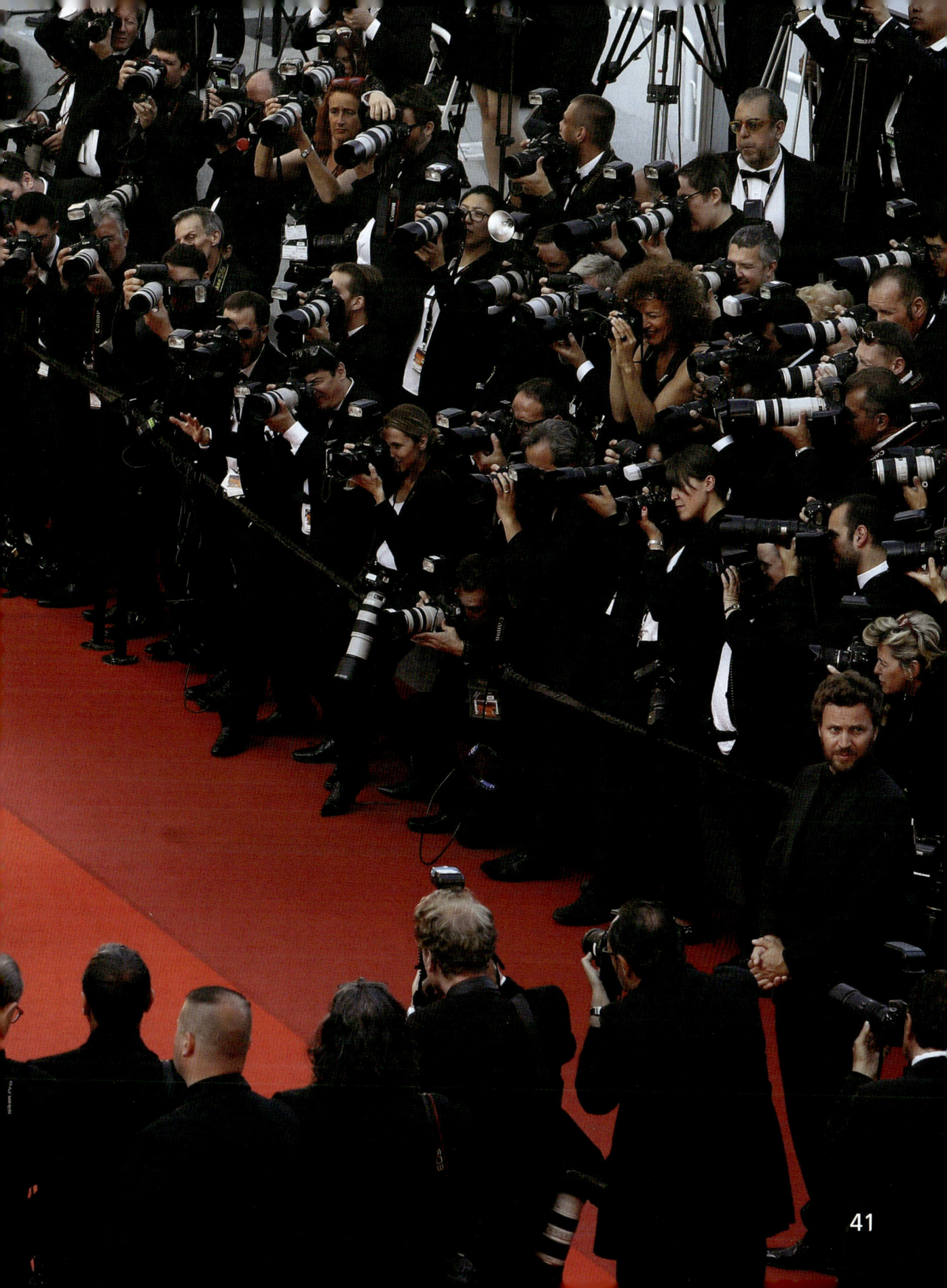

Movies for Everyone!

Making a movie is a long and complicated process involving many different people with very special skills.

Movies today are one of the main forms of entertainment all around the world. Hundreds of new films are made each year, and new stars appear on screen at the cinema, and all over the news and internet to promote their films. At a time with so much digital technology, it has never been easier to watch a movie.

Yet while many new movies will soon be forgotten, the really great movies will be remembered for a long time. Great stars, great scenes and a great script will always produce a great movie.

Thousands of movies are made by thousands of people about many subjects, from space exploration to imaginary worlds under the sea. People watch movies that were made with the latest special effects, but they also enjoy movies for decades after they were made.

Glossary

adversity	difficulty
computer graphics	effects and pictures made with a computer
debut	first appearance or showing
ecological	relating to looking after the planet
epic	long and often involving a hero or heroine
exploded	increased very fast
fantastical	from one's imagination
fairy tales	traditional stories for children
feature film	long film, usually over an hour
industry	business
innovators	people who have new ideas and who try new things
latex	type of rubber
martial arts	sports related to self-defence and attack, often from countries in Asia
method	way of doing something
nominated	entered for an award

portray	show
project	shine onto a surface
special effects	sounds and graphics that help a movie seem real to the audience
still	photo or single shot from a film
studios	places where films are made
thwarted	prevented from doing something
trailer	short sample of film to see what it is like

Index

actor   7, 15, 19-21, 29-36, 39, 40

Anime   12, 13, 28

animation   10, 12, 13, 38

award   8, 17-19, 21, 23, 25, 44

Bollywood   8, 9, 18-20

China   8, 24, 25

camera   3-6, 14, 16, 22, 33, 34, 36

cartoon   5, 10, 12, 15, 30

director   7, 15 16, 22, 25, 32-34, 37

Hollywood   6-8, 14-16, 18, 22, 29

India   6-8, 14-16, 18, 22, 29

Japan   8, 12, 13, 28, 29

Nigeria   8, 22, 23

Nollywood   22, 23

stunt   27

USA   14, 23

Movie World — Colin Millar and Spike Breakwell

Teaching notes written by Sue Bodman and Glen Franklin

Using this book

Content/theme/subject
An extensive coverage of aspects of film and movie-making, this non-fiction book explores the historical development of the film industry through to the present day, and explains how a film is made. A mixed genre approach is adopted, including historical report and biography.

Language structure
- Appropriate grammatical devices are used to support the different text purposes, as in the use of fronted adverbials to denote the passing of time (*'Four years later ...'*, *'only 16 years after ...'*, p.5).
- Words and phrases, specific to the movie industry, are employed, such as *'Lights, camera, action!'* on p.3.

Book structure/visual features
- The various genre styles are clearly identified across different sections of the book, for example, in the historical reporting of early movie-making (pp.4-5)
- Photographs with appropriate captions support the main text.

Vocabulary and comprehension
- Topic-specific vocabulary (such as *'editing'* and *'trailer'* on p.37) is supported through non-fiction devices in the text or defined in the glossary.
- The author's vocabulary choices position the reader: *'He was so good ...'* (p.20); *'outstanding animations ... wonderfully imaginative stories'* (p.13).

Curriculum links
Science – Explore a range of scientific experiments related to photography and film, such as creating pinhole cameras and designing flick-book animations.

Literacy – Using the example of a film review on pp.38-39, children can write reviews of their favourite film, or of one that they didn't enjoy, giving personal reasons and seeking to persuade the reader.

Learning outcomes
Children can:
- recognise different non-fiction text types, exploring why a writer might choose to write in a particular genre for audience and purpose
- skim and scan text effectively to support fast research and recall
- identify features of biography, using them in their own writing.

Planning for guided reading

Lesson One: Exploring a range of text types
Give out a copy of the book to each child. Point out the title and ask: *What do you think this non-fiction book is going to be about?* Draw attention to the aspect of the global film industry which is a significant feature of the book. Explore the contents page and discuss the focus of each chapter. Activate children's prior knowledge by asking what text types they are likely to see: report, biography, explanation. Ask the children to read the introduction (pp.2-3) quietly to themselves, and then discuss their predictions for this book, and what they would like to find out.

Set an independent reading task: to read up to p.13. This section incorporates several different genre styles. As children read, ensure they are noticing how text features are used effectively to provide information – for example, note how pp.6-7 includes historical report, biography, a fact box and illustrations.

Bring the group together and discuss what they have learned about the early development of film-making, and its spread around the world. Evaluate layout in helping to provide information – such as the effectiveness of captions on pp.4-5 to support the main text.

Follow up after the lesson: Using the pages read so far, ask the children to create a timeline of the development of film, picking out key events and dates from the information in the text.